Pennsylvania Dutch Christmases

Customs in Berks, Chester Dauphin, Lancaster, Lebanon & York Counties

By
Gerry Kershner

PENNSYLVANIA DUTCH CHRISTMASES:
Customs in Berks, Chester Dauphin, Lancaster, Lebanon & York Counties

© 2007 Gerry Kershner

All rights reserved. Request reproduction permission
in writing from the author:
Gerry Kershner, PO Box 493, Ephrata, PA 17522

ISBN: 978-1-60126-079-6
Library of Congress Number: 2007938338

Masthof Press

219 Mill Road
Morgantown, PA 19543
(610) 286-0258 • www.masthof.com

DEDICATION

Dedicated to
James S. Morrison
who personally and through the
National Christmas Center
has brought the
joy of Christmas
to many children of all ages
through the years.

ACKNOWLEDGEMENTS

In addition to the acknowledgements made within the text and in the photo captions, the help of the following persons and organizations in reading and research is sincerely appreciated:

C. Richard Beam, Erwin Boettcher,
Catholic Diocese of Harrisburg, Ephrata Library,
Evangelical and Reformed Historical Society,
Jay A. Felty, Campbell Fitzhugh, Peter V. Fritsch,
Guthrie Memorial Library in Hanover,
Hamburg Area Historical Society,
Hershey/ Derry Township Historical Society,
Historical Society of the Cocalico Valley, Ken Kershner,
Kurt Kershner, Lancaster County Historical Society,
Lancaster Library, K. Varden Leasa, Lititz Library,
Manheim Historical Society, National Christmas Center,
Larry D. Newby, Reading Library, R. Ronald Reedy,
Dale Shelley, Byron Smith,
Tri-County Heritage Society, Doug Winne.
Special thanks to my wife, Flossie, for keyboarding, research, proofreading and helping in countless ways.
Any errors are the responsibility of the author.

FOREWORD

This work was prompted by reading the fortieth anniversary edition of Alfred Shoemaker's *Christmas in Pennsylvania* during the past Advent season. Shoemaker's book is excellent reading for those seeking a more scholarly approach, especially to the folk cultural aspects of Christmas.

This book is my modest attempt to share what I've learned about nineteenth century celebrations of Christmas in Lancaster and the surrounding counties. My primary sources were English newspapers and church periodicals because of my somewhat limited knowledge of the local Pennsylvania German dialect. (Although I was raised speaking the dialect, disuse for many years has taken its toll.) Many old photographs and postcards were also researched. Whenever possible I have tried to use original rather than secondary sources.

My hope and prayer is that you learn something new about our rich Pennsylvania Dutch Christmas heritage and find this brief work enjoyable. Only by understanding both the Christian and the secular roots of the holiday can we truly appreciate the real meanings of these Pennsylvania Dutch celebrations of Christmas. May all of us do our part to respect and preserve these traditions.

Gerry Kershner
Lititz Moravian Church Square
Easter Monday, 2007

CONTENTS

Acknowledgements 4
Foreword 5
1. INTRODUCTION 9
2. PUTZES, STARS, TROMBONES 13
3. OTHER CHURCHES 21
4. TREES 37
5. WOOLWORTH 49
6. CAROLS 53
7. CHRIST KINDEL AND OTHERS 57
8. TRIMMINGS 67
9. COOKIES 71
Index 79

*The Reformed Church Messenger, Dec. 21, 1893.
Courtesy of Evangelical and Reformed Historical Society.*

1. INTRODUCTION

Christmas, a shortening of Christ-mass, has been a Christian celebration from the very beginning in the fourth century AD. It is a celebration of the birth of Jesus Christ, as written in Luke 2:4-7 of the King James Bible, the English version commonly used up to the early twentieth century:

And Joseph also went up from Galilee, out of the city of Nazareth, into Judea, unto the city of David which is called Bethlehem (because he was of the house and lineage of David) to be taxed with Mary his espoused wife, being great with child. And so it was, that while they were there, the days were accomplished that she should be delivered. And she brought forth her firstborn son, and wrapped him in swaddling clothes, and laid him in a manger because there was no room for them in the inn.

This primary Christian significance of Christmas is not a denial of the many non-Christian influences, such as the winter solstice celebration, that have also been present from the very beginning and continue up to the present. We will be looking at both the Christian and secular Christmas traditions as they were expressed in the Pennsylvania Dutch (really Dietsch/German) country. While focusing on the nineteenth century when these local Christmas traditions were strongest, late eighteenth century beginnings and traditions that remained into the early twentieth century are included.

Perhaps surprisingly, many of the early settlers in the area now known as the Pennsylvania Dutch country did not celebrate Christmas during the eighteenth and nineteenth centuries. Like the Puritans of New England, many of these early settlers found no biblical basis for celebrating the birth of Jesus Christ. These groups included the Amish, Brethren, Dunkards, Ephrata Cloister, Mennonites, Methodists, Presbyterians and Quakers. Many of these early settlers came to Pennsylvania to escape religious persecution in their homelands. For the most part they had a strong Christian faith but rejected the celebration of Christmas along with other rituals of the Roman Catholic Church.

Conversely, the few Roman Catholics and the more numerous liturgical Protestants, who followed a stricter order of worship and a yearly church calendar, generally celebrated Christmas and other Christian holidays. They tended to bring their Christmas traditions along with them and plant them in Pennsylvania soil. Catholics celebrated Christmas using the Mass. The liturgical Protestants included Episcopalians, Lutherans, Moravians and German Reformeds. Their traditions included decorating churches with greens, Advent hymns and Christmas carols, Christmas trees, Christmas communion and other traditions focused on celebrating the birth of Jesus Christ.

But many European immigrants also brought other traditions that were outside of the authority of the churches and were sometimes even condemned by the churches. Looking at these folk traditions will help us understand the uniqueness of the nineteenth and early twentieth century Pennsylvania Dutch Christmases.

The Moravians probably brought the strongest Christmas traditions with them and had rather sophisticated Christmas celebrations even in the late eighteenth century. Our attention will then focus on the Roman Catholics and Protestant groups that celebrated Christmas, including the Lutherans and German Reformeds.

After taking a good look at Christmas trees, we'll take brief looks at F.W. Woolworth's contribution to Christmas and Christmas carols. We'll also try to unravel the roots of Christ Kindel, Kriss Kringle, Saint Nicholas, Santa Claus, Belsnickel and mummers.

The Pennsylvania Dutch country has always been known for good cooking and good baking; Christmas was not an exception. So we'll look at a sampling of typical turn-of-the-century Christmas recipes in closing.

2. PUTZES, STARS, TROMBONES

While many of the early settlers in the Pennsylvania Dutch country didn't celebrate Christmas, others brought their Christmas traditions along with them. Not only in Pennsylvania, but also throughout the colonies, the Moravians were noted for their very special Christmas celebrations from the earliest years. They were generally more enthusiastic about celebrating Christmas than any of the other Christian groups from the earliest times.

While the Moravians spoke German, they didn't consider themselves a part of the plain groups or the gay Dutch. While the plain groups and gay Dutch had come to Pennsylvania to escape religious persecution in Europe, the Moravians came primarily to do missionary work among the American Indians. And they simply brought their well-established Christmas traditions along with them. One of those traditions is the putz.

PUTZES

The putz was brought from Europe to Pennsylvania by the early Moravian settlers. Putz is a German word that means decoration or ornamentation. It is a miniature representation of the manger scene in Bethlehem at the very minimum. A putz usually includes a portrayal of the shepherds and their sheep as described in Luke 2:8 (KJV):

And there were in the same country shepherds abiding in the field, keeping watch over their flock by night.

Matthew 2:1 (KJV) provides the basis for including the wise men in most putzes, usually riding camels:

Now when Jesus was born in Bethlehem of Judea in the days of Herod the king, behold, there came wise men from the east to Jerusalem.

Other biblical scenes related to the birth of Jesus may also be included such as the angel visiting Joseph (Matthew 1:20). Mary visiting Elizabeth (Luke 1:39-45), giving of the gifts by the wise men (Matthew 2:11) or the flight into Egypt (Matthew 2:13-14).

Miniature of Moravian Church Square made in 1847 by Rev. Peter Wolle and Ferdinand Rickert for church putz. Courtesy of Lititz Moravian Church.

While replicas of local buildings (barns, bridges, churches, houses, or mills) might also be included, the primary focus of a true putz was always and remains the manger scene along with other biblical scenes. Originally the putz consisted of clay or wooden figures in a natural setting.

The putz has proven to be a good way to teach children about the Christmas story. Sermons in the early days of the Moravian Church often stressed the importance of children helping to prepare the family putz.

Nineteenth century Moravian families made trips into the surrounding forests as early as September in search of moss, ferns, gravel and stones of various sizes. Fathers generally were in charge of building the putz and making the buildings. Mothers taught one of the children to narrate the presentation.

On Christmas Eve families would go to a candlelight service at the church and then go home to the putz. One child would narrate the Christmas story and the father would light a candle to illuminate each scene resulting in a roomful of light by the end of the story. Then the family would enjoy a Christmas dinner and exchange gifts.

A putz should not be gaudy, but should instill a hush of reverence and silent contemplation about the birth of the Son of God.

*Pre-1929 Christmas interior with star.
Courtesy of Lebanon Moravian Church.*

STARS

Moravian stars only really gained popularity among non-Moravians in the latter part of the twentieth century. In all probability the many-pointed Moravian star, occasionally called the Advent star, originated about the middle of the nineteenth century as a geometry exercise in a Moravian boarding school in Germany. Making the stars soon became a part of the handcraft program of the school.

By 1880 Peter Verbeck, a former student, began making and selling the stars and later his son, Harry, set up a shop in Herrnhut. Many of these stars found their way to Pennsylvania. The shop was closed by the First World War and some Moravians in Winston-Salem, North Carolina started producing the stars.

The traditional color of the stars is white and for many years they were only made of paper. Today they can be found in paper, plastic and various metals. The size and number of points of the stars varies, although the 26 point star is the most popular by far.

Traditionally the Moravian star was displayed from the first Sunday in Advent to the sixth of January, the twelfth day of Christmas. It is a reminder of the star seen by the wise men:

Where is he that is born King of the Jews? For we have seen his star in the east, and are come to worship him (Matthew 2:2, KJV).

The Moravian star also serves as a reminder of Jesus, whose birth is being celebrated. In Revelation 22:16 (KJV) he says of himself:

I am the root and the offspring of David, and the bright and morning star.

Trombone Choir in the church belfry, 1904.
Courtesy of Lititz Moravian Church.

TROMBONES

Music has always been an important part of Moravian Christmas celebrations. The Moravians brought many Advent and Christmas hymns along with them from Europe.

The Lititz Moravian congregation celebrated their first Christmas Eve service for children in 1759 and used candles at this service for the first time in 1765. Trombones were used for the first time as a part of the Christmas Vigil Service by the Lititz congregation in 1771 using a recently purchased set of trombones.

The Hebron Moravian congregation in Lebanon County also celebrated Christmas in the eighteenth century with full orchestra, trombones and choir. The children received lighted wax candles and apples on Christmas eve. The church was always decorated with evergreens and the school room had its putz.

Through their music and in many other ways, the Moravians have been a significant influence on the development of Christmas celebrations in Pennsylvania as well as the rest of the country.

The Manheim Sentinel of December 24, 1852, carried the following interesting article about Christmas Eve in Lititz: The religious celebration of Christmas Eve at Lititz is simple and peculiar. At the appointed hour the service of the church will commence with instrumental music by the choir, after which the Pastor will read the sacred history of the birth of Christ, when all will partake of the Love Feast, consisting of a "Love Feast Cake" and a mug of hot coffee. The choir will again perform a piece of sacred music, near the conclusion of which all the little children will be served with a lighted wax candle about four inches long which they will hold in their hands until the close of the ceremony.

Christmas, 1901.
Courtesy of Lancaster Moravian Church.

3. OTHER CHURCHES

As mentioned in the introductory chapter, Catholics and liturgical Protestants generally brought their Christmas traditions with them and planted them in Pennsylvania soil. Catholics celebrated through the mass and Protestant groups celebrated through communion. Some of the other Protestant groups started recognizing Christmas toward the end of the nineteenth century. The following excerpts and photos give a general overview of churches during the late nineteenth and early twentieth centuries.

The Lancaster Daily Evening Express of December 24, 1858, carried the following interesting notice: A beautiful Christmas tree has been put up in St. Paul's M.E. Church in South Queen Street by Mr. Wm. Hensel which will be exhibited tomorrow. The price for admission (ten cents) to be appropriated towards aiding in extricating the church from its present financial troubles.

By December 29, 1860, the following was reported in *The Columbia Spy*: Christmas day was taken full advantage of as a holiday in our borough. All places of business were closed and the churches well attended. The Episcopal and Catholic churches were handsomely decorated with green, according to custom.

Pre-1895 Christmas.
Courtesy of Trinity Lutheran Church, Mount Joy.

On December 27, 1866, *The Columbia Spy* reported: The Sunday School children of St. Paul's Episcopal Church had a delightful time on Thursday afternoon. The church has been more tastefully decked this Christmas than it has ever been before. On Thursday a tree was put up and loaded with good and tasty things for the children. At three o'clock the children, together with some of their parents and friends, assembled in the church and for an hour and a half were as happy as could be. The singing of the children was excellent. We always rejoice at the occurrence of such meetings, since their effect is to everyone good.

The Oxford Press of December 19, 1866, reported the following: The Fair and Festival at Oxford Hall, on Christmas afternoon and evening, for the benefit of the United Presbyterian Church, promises to be a fine entertainment, and we hope will be well patronized by the public at large. The object to which the funds are to be applied is a most worthy one, and those who bestow their patronage will be consoled with the reflection that their Christmas change has been well spent. The fairs and festivals heretofore held in the Hall have been so well attended and so productive of good social feeling and enjoyment that the managers of the present arrangement feel confident of full success. Then, let one and all attend.

On December 30, 1876, *The New Holland Clarion* gave the following account: REFORMED SUNDAY-SCHOOL ANNIVERSARY. — For the last ten years past the Anniversary of the Reformed Sunday-School has been one of the most interesting features in the Christmas festivities of New Holland, and the anniversary just celebrated has, in the main, been fully as interesting as any previous one. The first thing to greet the eye on entering the church was a handsome Christmas tree standing in front of the pulpit, and tastefully decorated with various ornaments, candies, festoons, flags, &c., while underneath the tree stood a large doll, natural as life almost, piles of stockings filled with candies and "Gloria in Excelsis," in letters of evergreen.

*Late nineteenth century Christmas.
Courtesy of Brickerville United Lutheran Church.*

The Columbia Spy of December 20, 1873, made the following announcement: The Reformed Church of this place, will, according to custom, hold a festival on the coming Christmas. The morning services will commence at 6 o'clock. On Christmas evening a festival will be given for the children, to consist of singing, dialogues and addresses. A large Christmas tree is also being prepared, which will add much to the pleasure of the occasion. All are cordially invited.

On January 2, 1875, the following news was reported in *The Columbia Spy*: On Christmas morning about 4 o'clock, the colored people, who held services during the night in the A.M.E. Church made their accustomed round singing characteristic hymns in our streets. Later in the morning services were held at the Reformed Church, U.B. Church and in the Roman Catholic churches.

St. Michael's Lutheran Church, Strasburg, 1906. Author's Collection.

The following announcement was printed in the December 25, 1875, issue of *The Columbia Spy*: The Reformed Congregation will hold an early Christmas morning service in the church, consisting of music and addresses by the Revs. John McCoy and C. Clever. A musical performance will be held by the choir with the Hummelstown Cornet Band, consisting of sacred melodies and hymns suitable to the occasion, commencing at 5:45 o'clock, a.m. Christmas services to commence at 6:00 o'clock, a.m.

The Columbia Spy of December 25, 1875, also announced: The Roman Catholic Churches — St. Peter's on Second and Trinity on Cherry — are ready for the great festival, which this church observes with greater ceremony than any of the other Christian churches. Both edifices have been decorated and Mass will be celebrated at different hours.

The following article was found in the December 31, 1877, *Lancaster New Era*: Old Donegal Church. The Sunday school connected with this time-honored church will hold their first Christmas entertainment on Saturday, the 29th inst. The exercises commence at one o'clock p.m.

On December 31, 1877, *The Lancaster New Era* reported the following: The Sunday school festival which was held in St. John's church, Marietta, on Thursday afternoon was indeed a happy occasion for all the little folks of the parish.

Bethany Reformed Church, Ephrata, 1909.
Courtesy of The Historical Society of the Cocalico Valley.

The beautiful edifice was handsomely decorated with the evergreen — spruce, laurel, ferns and Florida moss — and the radiant faces of over two hundred children.

On December 20, 1878, *The Lititz Record* announced: The Sunday-school connected with the James Coleman Memorial Chapel above Brickerville will hold appropriate Christmas exercises on Thursday afternoon, December 26, The programme will be an interesting one.

On December 23, 1882, *The Columbia Spy* carried the following Christmas announcement: In Mr. Darmstetter's German Evangelical Lutheran Church, on Locust Street, there will be appropriate religious observances of the festal occasion, both by the congregation and the school.

On December 26, 1885, *The Columbia Spy* reported: In the Catholic churches there will be masses at the usual early hours. In St. Peter's at 5:00 and 9:00 a.m. The services in this church, at both hours, will be of an excellent character. Farmers' Mass will be rendered by a full choir of well-trained voices. The church is beautifully decorated, the alter being one grand bouquet of flowers. In Holy Trinity, mass will be celebrated at 6:00, 8:00 and 9:45 a.m.

The following announcement appeared in *The Reformed Church Messenger* of January 9, 1896: Rev. Morgan A. Peters, York. On Christmas evening Zion Church was not large enough; because of the increase in the Sunday school it was half filled with scholars. "The Morning Star," was rendered in fine style. An orchestra of seven pieces accompanied.

The Reformed Church Messenger of December 31, 1896, reported the following from Reading: Rev. Dr. B. Bausman, pastor, St. Paul's. The church was elaborately and tastefully decorated with laurel. Regular services of the congregation, at 6 A.M. Large attendance. Sunday school services at 6 P.M.

The music, accompanied by an orchestra, was finely rendered, interspersed with a few short addresses, and recitations by the scholars.

The Reformed Church Messenger of January 12, 1899, reported the following from Spring City: The Sunday school of St. Vincent Reformed Church held their exercises on Christmas night. A special service was rendered, and was appreciated by a large audience. The usual gifts of candy were distributed. Offering $19.32, for Bethany Orphans' Home.

Trinity Lutheran Church, Ephrata, c.1909.
Courtesy of The Historical Society of the Cocalico Valley.

The Hershey Press of December 24, 1909, ran the following notice: The Union Deposit United Brethren Sunday School will hold their Christmas entertainment on Friday evening, December 24, at 7:30 o'clock. A splendid program has been arranged, consisting of music, vocal and instrumental, and recitations. Santa Claus will be there — direct from the North Pole.

Christmas, 1919, First Methodist Church, Columbia.
Courtesy of Charles R. Heim.

On December 30, 1891, *The Oxford Press* reported: Mt. Zion M.E. Sunday School held their annual Christmas entertainment on Christmas eve. Despite the gloomy weather the house was filled and the usual program was carried out.

*St. Mary's Croatian Catholic Church, Steelton, c.1920.
Courtesy of Catholic Diocese of Harrisburg*

The Hershey Press of December 24, 1909, ran the following notice under Campbelltown Briefs: The Union Sunday school is practicing for their Christmas festival, which will be held on Christmas Eve. A splendid program has been prepared, and a cordial invitation is extended to all to attend.

St. Lawrence German Catholic Church, Harrisburg, c.1920.
Courtesy of Catholic Diocese of Harrisburg

Christmas, c. 1915.
Courtesy of Trinity Evangelical Congregational Church of Lititz,
formerly known as United Evangelical Church of Lititz.

Especially in the early twentieth century it became more common for church functions to be held outside of the church. The following was reported in the December 16, 1915 *Oxford Press*: The bazar and luncheon held in Grange hall, Locust Street, last Friday and Saturday by the Ladies' Aid of Oxford M.E. Church cleared about $85. The hot chicken sandwiches and croquettes and fine sauer kraut dinner on Saturday were appetizing.

*Christmas at St. Vincent de Paul Catholic Church, Hanover, 1929.
Courtesy of Hanover Library.*

This very small sampling indicates that churches celebrated the Christmas holiday in a variety of ways during the late nineteenth and early twentieth centuries. There is no point in trying to impose an artificial uniformity to this growth of the celebration of Christmas. There were significant differences within denominations as well as between denominations. There were also differences between city churches and rural churches. Sunday schools, and therefore Christmas programs, came to the city churches first and then to the rural churches.

Trees were an important part of decorating for Christmas; we now turn our attention to Christmas trees.

4. TREES

Apparently the hanging of greens preceded the display of trees at least in the churches and probably also in homes. The Christmas tree was a custom brought to Pennsylvania by the early German settlers. An interesting article condensed below on the origins of the Christmas tree was printed in *The Columbia Spy* of December 22, 1883:

The Christmas tree is of German origin, but it has been thoroughly accepted and adopted in this country. The American Christmas is a modification, or rather combination, of English and German customs. The customs we have inherited from our ancestors have been harmoniously blended. There is every year more and more uniformity in the observances, until Christmas day, from one end to the other of the Union, presents the same joyful similarity. A marked feature of Christmas day next to its religious character, is its domestic nature. It belongs especially to the little folks. For He, whose birth it celebrates, taking upon himself the nature of a child, blessed little children, and declared that such was the Kingdom of Heaven.

The earliest written record of a Christmas tree is in the diary of Matthew Zahn from Lancaster. On December 20, 1821 he writes that "Sally and our Thomas and Wm. Hensel was out for Christmas trees, on the hill at Kendrick's saw mill."

We continue to encounter occasional mention of Christmas trees in newspapers and periodicals up through the Civil War, but following the war the occurrences become much more numerous. By the end of the nineteenth century the Christmas tree had been firmly established as a Christmas tradition in homes, churches, businesses and communities in the Pennsylvania Dutch country.

TABLETOP TREES

The first Christmas trees in Pennsylvania were decorated and displayed on top of a table. They were decorated with dried fruit, nuts, cookies, candy, handmade paper ornaments and candles. By the late nineteenth century blown glass ornaments were imported from Germany. Electric lights for the trees were available before the turn of the century but didn't become popular until the early twentieth century. Floor to ceiling trees became popular about the same time.

TREES IN HOMES AND SCHOOLS

Christmas trees became much more common in homes and schools following the Civil War. *The Lititz Record* of December 20, 1878, encouraged readers with the following words:

Feather tree, c. 1900.
Courtesy of National Christmas Center.

Everybody should put up a Christmas tree, which, besides being a great delight to the little ones, also amuses the big folks, who go from house to house, asking, "Kin I see your Christmas tree?"

Apparently the encouragement was heeded, because the next issue (December 27, 1878) reported: Christmas night presented another lively appearance on our streets. On this night it is the custom here — and has been ever since we can recollect — to go from house to house to see Christmas trees. Every place where Christmas trees were on exhibition there was an almost constant stream of people passing in and out.

*Pre-1908 tree in Washington Boro schoolroom.
Courtesy of Charles R. Heim.*

The New Holland Clarion of December 27, 1879, reported: In our public schools, Mr. T.H. Patton, principal and Mr. D.W. Dietrich, teacher of No. 2 school, each had very large and beautiful Christmas trees, elaborately and beautifully decorated, and also had the numerous pictures and mottoes which they have in their rooms, gracefully entwined with evergreens and fancy colored papers, the whole presenting a cheering scene.

Virginville School picture, Christmas, 1907.
Courtesy of Virginville Grange.

"The Family and the Christmas Tree"
from The Reformed Church Messenger of December 21, 1893.
Courtesy of Evangelical and Reformed Historical Society.

COMMERCIAL TREES

While individuals continued to search for and cut their own Christmas trees, *The Columbia Spy* started to report the availability of trees for sale by the late nineteenth century: A novel feature of the market house was the exposure for sale of Christmas trees, big and little, to suit the fancy and purse of the purchaser. (December 25, 1875) Harry Long says he has sold over 700 Christmas trees this season. (December 21, 1889)

COMMUNITY TREES

Community Christmas trees became quite popular after outdoor electric lighting had become feasible and relatively safe. By 1915 Harrisburg, Lancaster, Reading and York had community Christmas trees. But the smaller towns were not to be outdone as the following two examples attest.

OXFORD'S CHRISTMAS TREE

On December 16, 1915, *The Oxford Press* reported:

Days are flying and Christmas is almost here, so is the Community Christmas Tree. Out along the beautiful Octoraro in the woods of Mr. Roe C. Collins, Spruce Grove, a grand spruce tree of over 50 feet in height was located Saturday afternoon by members of the local committee and heads of the Electric Company.

On Monday afternoon the woods were visited and with five sturdy workmen of the L.O. & S. Railway the fine big spruce was leveled to the ground by a cross-cut saw in the hands of two competent sawyers and then a roadway was made to the public road, down which it is to be drawn to a car and then railroaded into Oxford. The snow favored this work greatly and the four big strong horses of Mr. Collins, with help of his men, block and tackle, landed the big tree at Spruce Grove station on Tuesday, after a stiff day's work in the snow and biting wind. Friends of the enterprise are coming forward with gifts of money in order to defray the expense connected with such a laudable message the tree will bear when placed in position, and hundreds of electric lights will shed forth their light, as a symbol of the love and joy abroad at this sacred season.

The magic which makes Christmas a pleasure and Christmas giving a joy is the honest, heartfelt love of Christmas and friends, and the wish to bring the happiness of the one into the hearts of others. Only so shall our Christmas be a happy one. Let us as loyal citizens enter into this community celebration in a true Christmas spirit.

The tree arrived in Oxford over the L.O. & S. Wednesday afternoon.

FIRST LITITZ COMMUNITY TREES

The first Lititz Community Christmas trees were erected on Memorial Square in 1915. This was a cooperative effort between Lititz Borough and the town's people. The Borough furnished the trees and the citizens provided the decorations. Each corner of Memorial Square was marked with a tree, plus a larger tree in the center, which was trimmed with garlands and lighted with 50 electric bulbs. Bunting in the Stars and Stripes pattern, was draped around the trees and across the front of Memorial Square giving the aura of a very festive Christmas season.

First Lititz Community Christmas Trees, 1915.
Photograph and short history courtesy of R. Ronald Reedy, Lititz historian.

*1912 Christmas tree from Lancaster Lyrics.
by David Bachman Landis © 1914.*

Cotton-wrapped tree, c. 1920.
Courtesy of National Christmas Center.

*Christmas party for patients, 1899.
Courtesy of The Reading Hospital.*

5. WOOLWORTH

Following his initial failure to establish a five cent store in Utica, New York in the spring of 1879, Frank Winfield Woolworth opened a store that was to become America's first successful "five-and-dime" at 170 North Queen Street in Lancaster on June 21, 1879. This very successful opening was quickly followed by a second, though short-lived, opening in Harrisburg on July 19 of the same year. A later store there proved profitable. Another short-lived attempt was the York store which opened the following year but lasted only three months, although again a later store proved successful.
In 1884 Woolworth opened a store in Reading in partnership with his cousin, Seymour Knox, which did well for many years.

So what do Woolworth's five-and-dime stores have to do with Christmas? Plenty! In the fall of 1879 a salesman persuaded Woolworth to purchase some glass Christmas tree ornaments even though he thought most of them would be broken before they were sold. They were the hit of the season and sold out in two days. Thereafter Christmas sales became a major role in the Woolworth success story. During Woolworth's first European buying trip in 1890 he discovered German hollow tree ornaments fashioned of blown glass and quicksilver in every conceivable color and shape. These also boosted Christmas sales until The First World War.

Woolworth was a big factor in commercializing Christmas and changing the seasonal buying habits of the working class. During the 1890's the ready-made glass tree ornaments, garlands, imitation greens and nativity sets were the rage. Later, in addition to the German tree ornaments, toys such as balls, dolls, teddy bears, sleds, toy trains and wagons became popular and helped Woolworth became known as "America's Favorite Christmas Store." An 1892 letter from Frank Woolworth concerning Christmas sales said: Give your stores a holiday appearance! Hang up Christmas ornaments. Perhaps have a tree in the window. This is our harvest time. Make it pay.

While sometimes pictured as being selfish, Woolworth must have been one of the first merchants to offer his employees a Christmas bonus in 1899. He even helped some of his former employers financially and helped many small suppliers to grow with his business, demonstrating the true spirit of Christmas. Woolworth paved the way for the developing modern customs for celebrating Christmas during the twentieth century not only in Pennsylvania but throughout America.

Woolworth Building, Lancaster c. 1912.
Author's Collection.

6. CAROLS

Advent hymns, Christmas hymns and Christmas carols had been used in many of the churches from the very beginning of Christmas celebrations in Pennsylvania.

The following interesting history of Christmas carols is condensed from the December 26, 1885, *Columbia Spy*: Christmas carols of a devotional nature were sung not only in the churches, but also through the streets, from house to house upon Christmas eve, and even after that morning and evening until the twelfth day. In those times men were able to spare more than one brief day for the celebration of Christmas, and kept up the festival for at least twelve days. Other carols were of a livelier nature, and were especially adapted to the revel and the feast. The carols were also called wassail songs, and probably originated among the Anglo-Normans. No Christmas entertainment was complete without the joyous singing of carols. Every guest at the table was expected to join in the carol.

Caroling on Christmas eve was always popular in the towns and cities of Pennsylvania. Organized caroling around the community Christmas tree only became a reality after the advent of the community Christmas tree in the early part of the twentieth century.

GLEN ROCK CAROLERS

Glen Rock Carolers in 1908.
Courtesy of Glen Rock Carolers.

In our constantly changing world it seems impossible that any tradition could be passed along from generation to generation for almost 160 years. Yet that's exactly what the Glen Rock Carolers have done. On Christmas Eve in 1848, Mark Heathcote, Charles Heathcote, Mark Radcliffe, George Shaw and James Heathcote with a bassoon decided to bless others in the community by singing traditional English carols.

All were relatives of William Heathccote, who had bought land in 1837 to build a woolen mill on the South Branch of the Codorus Creek. Radcliffe and Shaw were trained ropemakers, while the others worked in the woolen mill.

In 1848 they sang four songs brought from England: *Christmas Hymn*; *Hark Hark*; *Hosanna* and *While Shepherds*. Shortly thereafter, *Ye Faithful* was added. *Christmas Tree*; *Glory to God*; *O'Jesus Star of the Morning* and *Softly Sweetly*, American songs, were added in the 1890's. *Raise Christians, Raise*; *Silent Night* and *When Christ was Born* have been added since then.

At midnight the carolers begin their walk through the community, making various stops and concluding by singing the *Doxology* at the community Christmas tree shortly after daybreak. The singing has always been rendered in three-part harmony: lead, tenor and bass. Starting with James Heathcote's bassoon, the three-part singing has been accompanied by various string, woodwind and brass instruments through the years. Initially consisting only of five members, men have been added through the years within rather stringent guidelines. Presently the group has fifty members.

McCASKEY

J.P. McCaskey, the well-known Lancaster educator, made an important contribution to Christmas literature through the inclusion of many Christmas hymns, carols and songs in his wonderful Franklin Square Song Collections in eight volumes. It is said that the first American English translation of *Deck the Halls* was found in his first volume, published by Harper & Brothers in 1881.

7. CHRIST KINDEL AND OTHERS

DAS KRISCHKINDEL

by Henry Harbaugh

Ah, sweet Christmas-tide of childhood,
Warm and living in my heart!
Leaping pulses greet thy memory,
Tears upon my eyelids smart.
Dark the clouds, the years concealing,
Since I knew thee, as a boy;
But thou gleamest, bright as ever,
Fairest light of childhood's joy.

Some folks say it's all a fable —
There's no Christ Child. Maybe so!
Birds must pipe as birds are able.
Christian folk know what they know.
I have never seen Krischkindel
In the holy Christmas night;
But I've seen the tree asparkle
And I say: He caused its light.

(Edited and translated from
the Pennsylvania German
by Elizabeth Clarke Kieffer)

Christ Kindel (Christ Child in English, Christ Kindlein in standard German) is the earliest expression of a Pennsylvania Dutch bringer of gifts. Children were taught that Christ Kindel, riding on an old gray mule, would bring them gifts on Christmas Eve. Straw was left in the gift basket for the mule. Sometimes an older child, robed in white and carrying a basketful of gifts, impersonated the Christ Kindel. But everyone knew that the plates full of gifts on the table Christmas morning were left by the Christ Kindel during the night even if he did not make a personal appearance. During the first half of the nineteenth century Christ Kindel was a firmly established Pennsylvania Dutch tradition.

Christ Kindel was also used to designate the Christmas gifts from Christ Kindel or Christmas gifts in general as well as the gift bringer in the local dialect.

As the Pennsylvania Dutch became bilingual (English added to Pennsylvania German) through interaction and intermarriage, Christ Kindel became Kriss Kingel and eventually Kriss Kringle. This change did not happen without considerable opposition starting in the early nineteenth century and continued well into the late nineteenth century.

Of the many references in newspapers and periodicals opposed to this change, the following excerpt from *The Columbia Spy* of November 28, 1868, is typical: We have for many years observed that our contemporaries of Philadelphia and other places of equal celebrity in noticing the approach of Christmas, always write about "Criss Kringle," &c. Now we beg leave to say that there is no such thing as Criss Kringle. There is "Christ Kindlein" meaning the "infant Christ" and by corruption and ignorance of the German language it has been distorted into "Criss Kringle."

The publication and wide distribution in the Pennsylvania Dutch country of two books for children firmly established the use of the term Kriss Kringle despite the opposition. The books were *Kriss Kringle's Book* (Philadelphia, 1842) and *Kriss Kringle's Christmas Tree* (Philadelphia, 1845). By the late nineteenth century Kriss Kringle held his own, along with Saint Nicholas and Santa Claus, as the bringer of Christmas gifts, even in the Pennsylvania Dutch country.

Saint Nicholas, like Christ Kindel, was a real person. Nicholas was a Catholic saint born in the third century who served as Bishop of Myra in modern Turkey. His wealthy parents died while he was young and he gave his inheritance to help the poor, the sick and those who suffered. He loved children. His feast day is celebrated on December 6.

Following the American Revolution, New Yorkers promoted Saint Nicholas and on Saint Nicholas Day in 1809 Washington Irving published his satire, *Knickerbocker's History of New York*, with many references to a jovial Saint Nicholas character, not at all like the Catholic saint. By 1823 the poem, *A Visit from St. Nicholas* or *The Night Before Christmas*, by Clement C. Moore became extremely popular and was reprinted quite often in many of the local newspapers.

? Mr. & Mrs. Santa Claus ?
Photo by Hannah Wissler, 1914.
Courtesy of The Historical Society of the Cocalico Valley.

Thomas Nast's drawings from 1863 to 1886 established Santa Claus as cheery and chubby, wearing a fur-trimmed cap and coat, with a flowing beard and a long clay pipe.

As well as these rather obvious changes in appearance, somehow the name changed from Saint Nicholas to Santa Claus through the years, probably a natural phonetic change from the German *Sankt Niklaus* and Dutch *Sinterklaas*.

By the end of the nineteenth century Kriss Kringle, Saint Nicholas and Santa Claus were all being simultaneously and thoroughly accepted in the Pennsylvania Dutch country as well as the rest of the nation.

If at this point you are thoroughly confused by all this talk about Kriss Kringle, Saint Nicholas and Santa Claus, please relax! Be comforted by the fact that others over a hundred years ago were also apparently confused.

Wannamaker's of Philadelphia ran the following advertisement in *The Columbia Spy* of December 14, 1889:

St. Nicholas, Santa Claus, Kris Kringle are scrambling all over the store. The second floor is theirs equally with the first floor and basement.

DER BELSNICKEL
by Henry Harbaugh

O know you this terrible, this horrible man?
    Ho! — May we call him a person?
Yes, believe that he's real if you can,
    He looks to me too much like Satan!

Just look at his eyes, his nose — for all the world!
    His mouth opens wide like a shears;
A tail like an ox, yes, he's got one, not?
    And hairy fur like the bears.

If he comes to your house, there'll be plenty of noise,
    He looks for the naughty kids!
And finding one, he gets right to the point,
    And hammers those who backslid.

He stands right here with his dreadful rod,
    And growls his threats straightaway;
The children suddenly become real good
    And start right earnestly to pray!

Was one — as often the case is — real naughty;
    The whippersnapper who mocks his mother:
I bet he won't laugh at the Belsnickel's whip —
    He'll quickly beg for "good weather."

Now the Belsnickel shakes out his sack,
    Cookies and chestnuts for eating;
Who's good picks them up, — who's bad gets a whack!
    He really gets a good beating.

Now I learned something from the Belsnickel,
    This I will never forget:
According to how faithfully we sow
    The fruits of our work we'll get.

(Translated from the Pennsylvania German
    by the author)

Unlike Kriss Kringle, Saint Nicholas and Santa Claus, the concept of the Belsnickel, like the concept of Christ Kindel, is very local, being imported from Germany by the Pennsylvania Dutch. Belsnickel lore and practices changed considerably through the nineteenth and early twentieth centuries.

*The Hershey Press, c.1910.
Courtesy of The Hershey/Derry Township Historical Society.*

Belsnickel was originally Pelz-Nichol, or Nicholas in furs. The Belsnickel originally traveled alone and was a creature of terror and punishment. (Notice the demonic implications in the foregoing Harbaugh poem.) Dressed in outlandish garb and carrying a rod or whip, cookies and chestnuts were given to good children and punishment was meted out to those who did not learn their lessons and obey their parents.

Toward the end of the nineteenth century and into the twentieth century the Belsnickel seems to have become progressively more gentle and jovial, probably having been strongly influenced by Santa Claus.

There is still another aspect of the Belsnickel to be considered. From the mid-nineteenth century into the early twentieth century we read of people in groups masquerading or mumming on Christmas Eve, Christmas Day or Second Christmas. These groups also called themselves Belsnickels. While this was primarily an urban practice, it also spread out into the country.

Photo c. 1910 by Hannah Wissler labeled, "Santa Claus in Field." Courtesy of the Historical Society of the Cocalico Valley.

Mountain Springs Rifles, Ephrata, Christmas, 1900.
Courtesy of the Historical Society of the Cocalico Valley.

Mumming and masquerading at Christmas continued well into the early twentieth century. On December 24, 1909, Mary Reemsnyder, a teacher from Hinkletown, wrote in her diary, "Got many apples and cakes. Bessie, Cloyd, Chas. and I were out masquerading."

8. TRIMMINGS

No, not trimmings for trees or trimmings for turkeys. This chapter consists of interesting little tidbits about Pennsylvania Dutch Christmases that hopefully you'll enjoy.

ANIMAL TALK

An interesting folk belief that the Pennsylvania Dutch shared with many others outside of the area is that animals in the barn can talk on Christmas Eve. The details about who can hear and understand this talk seem to vary with the sources.

BARRING OUT THE SCHOOLMASTER

The custom of barring out the schoolmaster seems to have been practiced during the early and middle eighteenth century. Generally, the older students arrived early, locked themselves into the building and refused to open the door until the teacher agreed to their terms. After promising the pupils cakes, candy, nuts or a holiday the schoolmaster was allowed to enter the school.

CHRISTMAS WEATHER

Many Pennsylvania Dutch believed that if the ground was green on Christmas then it would be white on Easter and if it was white on Christmas then it would be green on Easter.

CHRISTMAS DEW

It was common practice for Pennsylvania Dutch farmers to throw hay in the barnyard so that the dew of Christmas Eve would fall on it. Then on Christmas morning it was fed to the cows and horses in the belief that the livestock would thrive during the coming year because of having eaten the hay soaked by the dew.

A comparable belief was practiced by their wives. They placed some bread outside safe from animals on Christmas Eve. In the morning the dew-soaked bread was divided among the family members before breakfast. It was believed the family would remain healthy throughout the year.

HOG BRISTLES

Butchering was often done prior to Christmas and this was fortunate for the boys and girls on the farms. Many of them would gather and clean the hog bristles that were scraped from the hides during butchering. Then they could sell them to a saddlemaker, brushmaker or the closest store. Sometimes they traded them for candy or something else they wanted at the store. Clean bristles sold as high as 75 cents a pound in the late nineteenth century.

Pre-1907 postcard, Pott's Store, Your Christmas Store, Ephrata. Author's Collection.

SECULAR CELEBRATIONS

Organizations other than churches also sponsored Christmas Programs. A report by *The Reading Eagle* of December 30, 1914, is typical: The members of Reading Nest, No. 2, Fraternal Order of Orioles, entertained several hundred children at the annual Christmas fete. A large Christmas tree, decorated with toys and candies, occupied a place in the center of the auditorium. There was a merry chatter of young voices as the little tots gathered around the tree and were handed gifts by Santa Claus.

SECOND CHRISTMAS

Second Christmas (December 26) was generally regarded as a day for relaxation and secular amusements such as fox chases, shooting matches, wheelbarrow matches, or corner ball. But there were also religious services.

On page 27 we mentioned the service held on December 26, 1878, in the James Coleman Memorial Chapel as announced in *The Lititz Record*. There are many other printed references.

The Lititz Express of December 30, 1887, reporting on Christmas at Manheim, said: On Monday all the banks, stores, mills and factories were closed. In the evening services were held by several Sunday schools.

As late as 1924, Estella Wanner's diary of December 26 included the following comments, "Jacob, David, Ethelbert, Mother and I attended church service. We came home and had a second Christmas dinner."

9. COOKIES

As mentioned in the introduction, the Pennsylvania Dutch country has always been known for good cooking and baking. The January 1, 1881 *New Holland Clarion* attests:

A grand and beautiful Christmas dinner is, of course, one of the necessaries on such an important occasion. Not the fatted calf, but the fattest turkey — or some other fowl equally as fat and good — that can be found is killed and prepared for feast, while every variety of side dishes, rich mince pies, toothsome cakes, and various et cetera too numerous to mention go to make a feast, such as our good Lancaster county housewives so well know how to prepare, and for which they have long since been famed throughout the land.

While space will not permit instructions for preparing a complete Christmas feast as described above, why not try some of the following typical early recipes this Christmas?

STUFFED DATES

This simple recipe for stuffed dates contributed by Mrs. Bortner was included in the *Third (1922) Edition of the Hanover Library Association Cookbook*:

Select rich, dark date, split one side and carefully remove the stone. In its place put quarter of English walnut, dip in granulated sugar and arrange on plate.

BACHELOR BUTTONS

The following recipe by Mrs. D.F. Stair was found in the *Third (1922) Edition of the Hanover Library Association Cookbook*:

10 ounces (2 1/2 cups) flour

10 ounces (1 1/2 cups) sugar

¼ pound butter

2 eggs

Mix butter and flour together, then add sugar and eggs, well-beaten. Make small balls, roll them in granulated sugar and flatten them a little. Bake on a well-greased tin.

My wife suggests making the balls about the size of a nickel and baking them for ten to twelve minutes in a 350 degree oven.

CANDIED ORANGE PEEL

The following recipe by Miss Blanche Hostetter was also taken from the *Third (1922) Edition of the Hanover Library Association Cookbook*:

One cup of sugar to the peel of two oranges. Cut the peel into thin strips and soak overnight in strong salt water. Wash it well in five or six waters to remove the salt and boil with sugar and one half cup of water for about ten minutes. Beat unit it sugars. Each piece should be separated before it hardens.

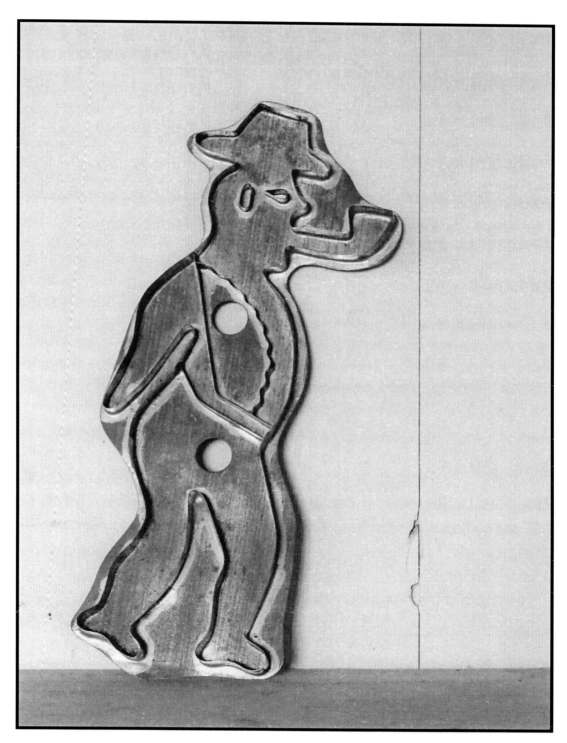

*Man with pipe reproduction cookie cutter over a foot high.
Courtesy of Karen Hurd, Tinsmith.*

MORAVIAN SUGAR CAKE

This recipe contributed by Mrs. R. Blickenderfer appeared in the *1905 Lancaster Moravian Church Cookbook*:

One pint home-made or one cent's worth baker's yeast, one pint milk (lukewarm), one cupful shortening, dissolved in one cupful sugar; work enough flour in the dough until it does not adhere to the fingers; let raise all night; spread on tins with hands (not too thick), let raise light; make butter holes; fill with soft butter, brown sugar and cinnamon and spread melted butter on top. Can also take one cake of Fleischmann's yeast to pint of milk; let them raise in the morning about one and one-half to one and three-fourths hours.

A handwritten note at the bottom of the recipe says, "Let raise all night — dissolve shortening in milk."

My wife used one ¼ ounce pack of Fleichmann's Active Dry Yeast in one pint of lukewarm whole milk. She used one cupful of butter mixed with one cupful of granulated sugar, working in seven cups of white flour. She let it raise overnight (about ten hours). In the morning she spread the dough in rectangular cake pans and let it set for about an hour. (Make butter holes about three inches apart so that cake can be cut into three inch squares after baking.) She baked the cake for thirty minutes in a 350 degree oven.

SAND TARTS

Sand tarts have been a popular Christmas cookie among the Pennsylvania Dutch for many years. The following recipe from Mrs. W.S. Alleman was found in the *Third 1922 Edition of the Hanover Library Association Cookbook*:

1 lb. sugar, ½ lb. butter, 1 lb. flour, 3 eggs

Cream butter and sugar, then add beaten eggs, then flour. Roll very thin, wash with yolks of eggs on top of tarts, sprinkle with cinnamon and granulated sugar.

Sand tarts are normally cut out with cookie cutters after being rolled very thin. Egg yolks are beaten and dabbed on top before being sprinkled with cinnamon and sugar mixed equally. Bake in a 350 degree oven for about fifteen minutes.

CRANBERRY JELLY

A recipe from *The Lititz Record* of December 20, 1878: Carefully wash and pick over two quarts of cranberries, add one pint of cold water, and place them in a porcelain-lined saucepan over a quick fire, stir occasionally, and when the berries are soft mash them thoroughly with a spoon, bring to a boil, and then add a quart bowlful of granulated sugar, boil ten minutes, and then pour into molds. The berries should not be on the stove more than twenty-five minutes, as the more quickly they are done the more brilliant the color of the jelly will be. Cool the molds with the cold water before using.

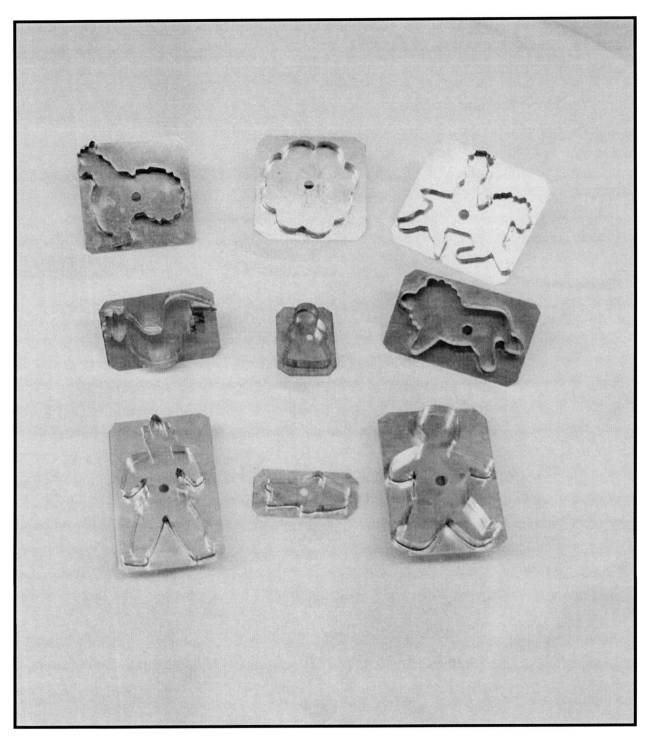

*Reproduction cookie cutters made from early patterns.
Courtesy of Charles R. Messner, Tinsmith.*

We close this little volume with verses from *Christmas Cakes* by David Bachman Landis in *Lancaster Lyrics* © 1912:

> Fresh Christmas cakes give good, crisp cheer
> When they come forth, just once a year;
> And, young or old folks think them best
> Of all bak'd cakes — these beat the rest.
>
> The baking time o' each December
> Was pretty prime, as we remember;
> Rare kitchen odors, always tempting,
> None could resist without relenting.
>
> We all lik'd cakes, whate'er their kind, —
> The ginger bread, e'en lemon rind;
> Square cakes, round ones, odd shapes or sort, —
> Each cake was ate with zest and sport.
>
> Making and baking things have chang'd,
> Somewhat as styles or sizes are rang'd;
> Though, yet, the same rich cakes are here,
> When Christmas comes, at close of year.

*Santa chocolate mold over two foot tall, c. 1920.
Courtesy of Wilbur Chocolate Company.*

INDEX

Advent 10, 17, 19
American Indian 13
Amish 10
Animal talk 67
Bachelor buttons 72
Barring out the schoolmaster 67
Belsnickel 11, 62-65
Brethren 10
Candied orange peel 72
Catholic 10, 11, 21, 25
Christ Kindel 11, 57, 58
Christmas carols 10, 11, 53-56
Christmas dew 68
Christmas tree 10, 11, 35, 37-48, 69
Christmas weather 67
Columbia Spy 21, 22, 25, 26, 28, 37, 43, 53, 59, 61
Commercial trees 43
Community trees 43
Cranberry jelly 75
Dunkards 10
Ephrata Cloister 10
Episcopalians 10
First Lititz community trees 45
German Reformeds 10, 11
Glen Rock Carolers 54-55
Harbaugh, Henry 57, 62, 64
Heathcote, Charles 54
Heathcote, James 54, 55
Heathcote, Mark 54
Heathcote, William 55
Hershey Press 30, 32, 64
Hinkletown 66
Hog bristles 68
Hurd, Karen 73
Irving, Washington 60
Jesus Christ 9, 10
Kieffer, Elizabeth Clarke 57
King James Bible (KJV) 9, 13, 14, 17
Knickerbocker's History of New York 60
Kriss Kringle 11, 59, 61, 63
Kriss Kringle's Book 59
Kriss Kringle's Christmas Tree 59
Lancaster Daily Evening Express 21
Lancaster Lyrics 46, 77
Lancaster New Era 26
Lititz Express 70
Lititz Record 27, 38
Lutherans 10, 11
Manheim Sentinel 19
Masquerading 65, 66
Mass 10
McCaskey, J.P. 56
Mennonites 10
Messner, Charles R. 76
Methodists 10
Moore, Clement C. 60
Moravian 10, 11, 13, 15, 17, 19
Moravian sugar cake 74
Mountain Spring Rifles 66
Mummers, Mumming 11, 65, 66
Nast, Thomas 61
New Holland Clarion 23, 41, 71
The Night Before Christmas 60
Old Donegal Church 26
Oxford's Christmas tree 43-44
Oxford Press 23, 31, 34, 43
Presbyterians 10
Puritans 10
Putz 13-15
Quakers 10
Radcliffe, Mark 54, 55
Reading Eagle 69
Reemsnyder, Mary 66
Reformed Church Messenger 28, 29
Saint Nicholas 59, 60, 61, 63
Sand tarts 75
Santa Claus 11, 30, 59, 61, 63, 64, 69
Second Christmas 65, 70
Secular Celebrations 69
Shaw, George 54, 55
Stars 16-17
Stuffed dates 71
Tabletop trees 38
Trees in homes and schools 38
Trombones 19
A Visit from St. Nicholas 60
Wannamaker's 61
Wanner, Estella 70
Winter solstice 9
Wissler, Hannah 60, 65
Woolworth, F.W. 11, 49-51
Zahn, Matthew 37

PENNSYLVANIA DUTCH CHRISTMAS IDEAS: